TAKING
Risks

Judith McDaniel

for Ann —
who showed me
how to take some of
these risks — thanks!

Judith

RISING
TIDE
PRESS

Rising Tide Press
PO BOX 30457
Tucson, AZ 85751
520-888-1140

Printed in the United States on acid-free paper.

Cover art by Jude Ockenfels

First Printing: May 2001

      McDaniel, Judith
      Taking Risks/Judith McDaniel

ISBN 1-883061-38-5

Library of Congress Control Number: 2001 132071

ACKNOWLEDGEMENTS

An early version of the Preface of this manuscript was originally published in *The American Voice*, No. 17, Winter, 1989.

"Santa Cruz del Quiche" was originally published in *Basta*, July 1990. Basta is the national journal of the Chicago Religious Task Force on Central America.

"Love Poem III and V" were originally published in *The Arc of Love*, edited by Clare Coss, New York: Scribners, 1996.

"Love Poem I and II" were originally published in *My Lover is a Woman*, edited by Leslea Newman, New York: Ballantine Books, 1996.

"Grand Canyon" was originally published in *Southwest Women Writers*, edited by Caitlin Gannon, Tucson, AZ: Javelina Press, 1996.

DEDICATION

For Jan

TABLE OF CONTENTS

PREFACE: TAKING RISKS

It is ironic. Sanctuary is about living dangerously. Sanctuary is about taking risks beyond the ordinary. Risks of class security or race security. Risks of the heart. Physical risks. I have never in my life felt as secure in myself as during those twenty-nine hours of captivity on the Rio San Juan. I knew well I might be killed. But I also knew more clearly than I had ever known before that I was in the right place. I was in the right place in that jungle and I was in the right place in myself. Taking the risk allowed me to be the person I had always wanted to be.

Sanctuary: A Journey, 1987.

I wrote that paragraph after my return from a trip to Nicaragua in 1985 a trip during which my Witness for Peace delegation had been fired on by U.S. backed Contras, held in the jungle of Costa Rica for twenty-nine hours, and then released to a chorus of disbelief from the U.S. State Department officials who suggested we had kidnapped ourselves. I gave talks all over the country on my return to try and counter that lie and at the same time explain what it was I had been hoping to accomplish down there in the jungle. "What is this about?" was a question I had indeed asked myself as I prepared for the trip, while I was a captive being marched at gunpoint through knee deep jungle mud, and as I tried to understand the full range of implications the trip, capture, and release had for me both personally and politically. I understood it had been important for me to take that risk, but I wasn't sure I knew why.

Taking risks, it has been suggested to me, is a literary cliche, the stuff of undergraduate poetry workshops. Or, I've been told, taking risks is what those early feminists did in the sixties and seventies, and our job now is not to take risks, but to consolidate our access into the system.

But I am convinced that we need to continue the discussion of risks, perhaps reminding ourselves now and then that the original meaning of risk was "danger and loss." The risks I refer to are the risks that lead to a profound change in our landscape, both the emotional landscape of our lives and the physically present landscape. Not all risks turn out well. We don't always return from a risk; some perish. And even when we return, it is possible that we have encountered an enormous loss as a result of taking the risk, one that will be with us as long as we live. But we go on in spite of that reality, in spite of our fear.

"I want to write down everything I know about being afraid," writes Audre Lorde, "but I'd probably never have enough time to write anything else. Afraid is a country where they issue us passports at birth and hope we never seek citizenship in any other country." Lorde is writing in *A Burst of Light* about her experience of living for the previous three years with cancer of the liver, but the image holds true every time we risk traveling past the boundaries set for us by a misogynist or racist or homophobic society. Every time we choose a risk, we are traveling outside of the limitations—real or perceived—of our lives. When we choose a risk, we are choosing to face down a fear, or at least to walk with it past the boundaries of our previous experience.

The poems in this volume vary in the type of risk they portray, but for me each of these areas represents the essential elements of risk taking—the potential for loss or gain, the feeling of danger, the opening of a new horizon.

Love is the first risk we take. Loving is the risk we have to be willing to take in order to encounter any of those things that allegedly come to us in maturity: the ability to experience intimacy, to grow in personal and spiritual complexity and joy, to engage in honest dialogue, to make art. Loving expands our heart space the borders of that country where we are issued passports at birth, that country where myths of safety keep us from experiencing our own lives. And because those of us who are lesbian or gay have been taught to deny to ourselves who we are and second to maintain silence about who we are and how we love, for us, risking love openly, daring to tell our stories openly, and witnessing our own lives become a crucial and central feature of our growth and survival.

Breaking that silence, however, can also put us in physical danger perhaps a more obvious risk at first than simply daring to love. Physical risks are the obvious ones. When a contra was pointing a rifle at me in Nicaragua, I knew I was at risk. Climbing in the Grand Canyon in any season is a physical risk. The boy we found shivering and abandoned at the bottom of the canyon could have been one of the many casualties of that landscape that is so awesome and so unforgiving of mistakes. Watching over my shoulder in Guatemala for a car with smoked glass windows as I walked with the brother of a refugee in Sanctuary in the United States, I knew I was at risk. But a friend who came home from war torn Central America to have her child in the safety of her familiar community, among friends and family who could help, talked with me about the absolute "democracy of injustice" when her much desired, much loved newborn drew a dozen breaths and then died. Physical risk? Emotional risk? Yes. And losing like this, being left alive to accept and understand the hard lessons that accompany risk, is also one of the outcomes that moves us past the borders of our previous experience.

Sometimes art itself is the risk that makes it possible for us to face the fears that are inhibiting our journey. I do not advocate art as therapy or presume that every self-expression that may be therapeutic is therefore art, but I have found that poetry and fiction are excellent places to begin to walk past the boundaries of our lives. The explosions and flying shrapnel of our emotional lives are not usually fatal in art.

And the risk we experience when we tell our stories truly is the risk of change: the risk that we will be changed by the telling and the risk our audience similarly experiences, that they will be changed by the hearing. In some traditions, this kind of truth telling is called witnessing. In others, it is called fiction or poetry. Living these poems has changed me, and I offer them to the reader with that warning.

Judith McDaniel

Grand Canyon

THE RIM

Have faith in me
I am the world's smallest traveling altar.
I am the altar and the door,
The prayer and the yearning

Marilyn Chin, *The Narrow Roads of Oku*

We travel for a long time toward this place
across the blackened volcanic hills
through scrub pine holding to bedrock
under the narrow dirt
past scraps of snow lingering on tundra.

And then it comes so suddenly,
the blink of an eye, one last step toward the edge
and we are staring down at all creation, the depths
out of which all life
the source
the beginning.

I stand astonished,
shaken at the raw and vulnerable rock
yawning awake before me.

CLIMBING DOWN

In the first hour of the descent
the lower legs take the strain,
the calves begin to ache

anticipation of nine more hours
climbing downward. The second hour
is slower, even the pain

moves up the thighs more slowly.
Gripping at rock through leather soles
burns my toes. In the fifth hour

we begin the Cathedral Stairs
winding north, then south, on switchbacks
tortured out of rock fissures,

stepping down one rock, then another,
heading at one moment directly back,
it seems, to where we began
only a few yards lower. Now my legs
tremble to the bone when I stop moving.

I pause to look back and up
and realize I have descended
into the cathedral. Above me rise
the spires of what is possible beyond imagining
lava cooled as it shot out of the earth,
pressed into permanence.
After the switchbacks a long path moves straight down
the talus slope. I walk on, past flowering cactus
and purple sage, small wildflowers in the cranny of rock,

---

down and down to the river. We have
been climbing down for nine hours.

Have you ever 'hit the wall' in your running?
my friend asks. I haven't. I know I've never pushed
that hard. Today I hit it over and over, imagine
each time I am smashing into my absolute
physical limit, but I cannot stop
this descent

and so I go on.

THE WALL

We sit under a ledge while the rain seeps into our skin
from the rock behind our backs. My hair has been wet
for two days and my fingers are washtub wrinkled.

Surrounded by rock I stare hard at the canyon wall,
looking for patterns, directions. Monsters
stare back from the dripped lava mud and canyon squirrels

flit in and out of caves, finding impossible perches
on edges of nothing. On the rim a stone eagle rises
toward flight and—as I stare—a dinosaur with open mouth

lurches from the rock. A million years of activity
carve that rough wall. Hour after hour
I sit silent, let the noise within

merge with the canyon wind and the spiral fall
of the canyon wren's call and the drip of mist
as it becomes a rocky stream. I look

into the wall's ancient cipher and see
myself. I am alone.
No companionship could breach these walls.

Here. Now. My shoulder leaning into this wall
is deception, the wall is my shoulder, my hand is
the wall which builds walls around me, smooths wetness

into my stone lungs, hardens my lava mud skin.
How should I ever dream that I could share
the breath of a star or feel on this rockface

the canyon wren's feather fall? There is terror
in the finality of a body. It is what it is,
as the rock is not the squirrel, so with each

succeeding age we have lost a bit of that
which bound us together, allowed our edges
to merge, leaving only that last miracle—

birth—which binds our form until death.
The return seems impossible: to dismantle
rock by rock this terrible finality, alter

this lonely individuality, believe that I
could stare into the wren's dark eye until I fall,
lost, into her depths.

COMING BACK OUT

We sit under that ledge for a day
and a night and when the black drizzle

grays, we pack up and start
the climb out. My friend says

the key is our pace and she leads us
slowly, our footsteps steady as

heartbeats. Packs weighing
like the world above us press down

on our backs. I try not to look up
not to imagine the nine miles ahead

our destination hidden in the mist
and clouds above. For the first hour

I am sure the climb out is not
possible. My feet are bruised and raw

and the pack straps cut my shoulders
with the weight of seven days uneaten food,

a sleeping bag sodden with rain.
One foot, then the other. Eyes cast down,

I watch the pattern of rock beneath,
wonder at the glow of cactus flowers

in the icy sleet, the gray light.
Suddenly we turn around a rock ledge

and find three boys huddled under one
rain poncho. I want to walk on,

keep my focus on putting one foot ahead
of the other, but we stop, ask *what's wrong?*

Oh, he's tired, says he can't make it,
so we're going to leave him here and go
get our leader to come back for him.
And my pack strap broke so I'm gonna leave
my pack here too. We'll be back,
one assures us, then they head off. The boy
under the poncho shivers, smiles with some
embarrassment at his own weakness. I look
more closely and see the blue shadow
under the line of his lips, the tremor
shaking out from his body core. *Where*
is the leader who is coming back for you?
I want to know. Up there. He nods toward
the rim and wraps his arms around his chest
to hold the shaking. The guys said they'd
send a ranger in a helicopter for me,
that's what they do when people get stuck.

I have had the same fantasy this morning
so I try to be gentle as I tell him
to look at the fog swirling down, rolling
along the grass, wrapping itself around rock
faces and smothering the light. *My dad's*
the leader, he assures me, *he'll make*
the rangers come and get me. I am
angry now, angry at the interruption of my
meditation, the quiet repetition of step
upon step that was making the climb out
seem possible, angry at a leader who would
leave any child shivering in a wet t-shirt,
angry at this child who believes the impossible.

You're going to walk with us, we tell him
and pull out sweaters, dry socks, a candy
bar, and canteens of gatorade. He stumbles
for a while, his toes falling lower than
his heel, but gradually he recovers,
fed, warmed, accompanied, and bounds ahead
on the path, chattering, while I still plod,
placing one foot heavily in front of the other.

IN THE MORNING

I walk back out across the rim
staring down as a shaft of sunlight
tries to pierce the heavy clouds beneath.

Today I am looking down
at a place where I have been.

I have climbed in
and back out.

In late spring we expected
seven days like this morning on the rim
hot sun, a desert landscape
where water would be scarce.

We weighed each ounce of food and gear,
judged what was necessary,
what weight we could bear,
what could be discarded.

And yet we were unprepared. Rain,
then unexpected snow, overtook us.
We carried baggage we didn't need,
left behind gear we longed for.

Beneath me the canyon is silent,
covered in a dreamer's cloud swirl.
A puff of occasional wind moves the mist
in waves of thought.

I have lost friends and lovers,
lost children not of my blood and the parents
whose blood gave me this life. I have shed
pieces of myself as I walked across the landscape
toward this place,
shed the ways in which I knew myself:
names and work and place, none stood by,
and yet
something remains that was with me from the first
some impulse, some stance, some way of beginning
that roots this life against the precipice,
that curls—a tight fisted seed—waiting,
always waiting for the fire's clean sweep.

Crossing The Line

TAKING RISKS: THE RIVER POEMS

1.
she squinted against the sun
eyes half closed she
loved this moment

sliding toward the rapid
the decision made nothing
could stop her descent

she stood to see the river's current
grasping the oars watching
the foam swirl into patterns

there she nodded to herself
knowing now how to enter
which current to follow as she

approached the smooth round hump
of water leading into the heart
of the river nothing else

in her life ever let her in this far
allowed her to plunge toward the heart
of the current

once she went over the edge
there would be no return only the forward
momentum of the craft pitched

toward discovery the river let her know
herself the limits of her strength and nothing
in her life knows her as the river knows her

she dipped one oar
turned the boat toward the first rolling
wave and slid down the smooth dark tongue.

2.

Whirlpools
suck you in
and spit you out.

It is important
to keep your balance even
as you go down—

diving for the margins
won't help
nor panic.

You never intend
to get drawn in.
Your eyes were fixed

on a goal downstream
but rivers have
a direction

that is not yours.
You will rise again
to the surface, circling,

one level at a time
until you can see more
than sky and water.

You must
be ready to choose
the moment you exit

paddle hovering
then cutting down
to shoot you out

in your own direction.
If you leave this moment
to the river,

you will wallow
in an eddy, directionless,
paddling against the current.

_____

3.

She stood on a high bank watching the current
she was about to enter flung a stick
into the water and marked its journey

a straight line past the water-buried rock
just on the edge of a sucking hole
out of danger and into a fast river.

In life, she knew, following the path
of least resistance could wash her right
into trouble

and she watched the dark hole where
the river swirled eddied turned back on itself
as if forward movement never happened.

In life and on the river she had found herself
on that edge traveling swiftly past a rock
on the straight line that would shoot her free

only to catch the tip of an oar slide
off the line trapped moving backward
wallowing in a whirlpool straining

to get back out into the mainstream where
she could rush forward catch the moment
cut through the waves with a clean quick

cast of the oar create her own chosen
direction with a small efficient effort.
Standing silent on the bank

she marked the line again noted the pine tree
that would tell her she was safely past the rock
saw herself pulling slightly left

as she raced forward on the edge of the hole
following exactly the line she had chosen.

CROSSING THE LINE

There are no heroes here
in this San Antonio courtroom
where the Branch Davidians from Waco
are on trial, only eleven people
who look like my neighbors—
several young men whose suits don't fit
well, a gray haired chubby older man,
one woman in a dark print large collared
dress. I slide into a seat
on a bench marked PUBLIC directly behind
the bench labeled SKETCH ARTISTS
in front of the five rows for the PRESS

and try to print these perfectly mundane
faces, faces belonging to brothers and sons
and wife, on the images in my brain
religious fanatics with automatic rifles,
cultists who abused their children,
the Waco wackos. Who cared
if they died?

Q: What is your definition of a cult?
A: Well, I never heard of them before.

On the witness stand agent Evers describes
how he—fully armed, wearing a bullet-proof
vest beneath his black assault uniform—
came around a corner of the compound that morning,

(and this is important, that being different
enough can get you surrounded by men in black
pointing their guns at you)

and saw three men, also armed, pointing
their weapons at him.
Two bullets hit his vest,
a third went into his arm,
a fourth creased his shoulder,
sliding under the flesh of his chest
for twelve inches or so.
He shows the jury the holes in the vest
as photographs of his wounds are projected
larger than life
on a courtroom wall.

Q: What is that discoloration on the vest?
A: That is my blood.

For a moment the blood focuses
us on this young man, his moment
of glory—that he lay for three hours
bleeding in a ditch.

> At the Alamo,
> just around the corner
> from this Federal Court,
> the names of the heroes
> are inscribed on brass plaques.
> David Crockett. James Bowie.
> William Barret Travis who drew
> his sword to make a line in the dirt floor
> and said, "Those prepared to give
> their lives in freedom's cause,
> come over to me."
> One hundred and eighty-nine heroes who
> —when given the chance
> to surrender by the Mexican General
> Antonio Lopez de Santa Anna

—answered with a cannon shot
and died every one.

The seeds of Waco are here
at the old Alamo mission
planted next to the cottonwood tree
by missionaries who knew the right
way to live, the right
god to trust and proved
they were right by subjugating
anyone who was different
and then came Santa Anna
to subdue those who had subdued
and then

concealed in cattle trailers
pulled by two pickup trucks
seventy agents in black descended
that day

        to serve a search warrant

two helicopters hovered above
as they piled out of the trailers
according to rehearsal, armed
with handguns, rifles, and six
AR15 weapons that would fire
through two or three walls of the compound.

        In the Alamo museum
        is a model of the battleground
        that day in 1836.
        Boys' toy soldiers surround
        the four-foot thick walls
        as smoke rises from the toy

canons and horses fall, writhe
in mock death agony.

Today's battleground
is no less carefully drawn to scale
with walls and ditches, assault
vehicles, and the observation towers.
With a pointer, we are shown who ran
where and from where
the first shots
were fired.

In the hours just before dawn
the Mexican army came, fought
through the four foot thick walls
put to death
every armed defender
with grapeshot, musket fire, and bayonets.

Noncombatants were spared
including six women who were wives or servants,
an infant and five children.

Q: Who were the bad guys?
A: The men who were shooting at us.

And this was the seed that sowed
the fire that grew into the flames
that poured over the walls
consumed the towers
lay waste the living quarters
the children's classroom
exploded—finally—the weapons cache.
One bronze plaque on the Alamo wall
tells how Major Robert Evans,

Master of Ordnance,
was killed as he attempted
to ignite the stored gun powder
and blow up the fort,
killing defenders and attackers.
All of the heroes of the Alamo
agreed to die by their own explosives.

There is no record of the votes
of the noncombatants —
Susanne, Gertrudis, Juana,
Ana, Trinidad, Petra,
and their children.

I wonder whether David Koresh
drew a line on the floor
with his sword
invited his followers to choose life or death.
I wonder if those surrounding the compound
with guns
would have spared the noncombatants.

In the courtroom are people
who would call David Koresh a hero
and those who would call him monster.
We sit side by side on narrow benches,
breathe the stale air under the watchful eyes
of TV cameras and federal marshals.
At each break, we stretch
our legs in the hall
and the men and women of the press call
home the news in mellifluous, fateful voices,
and for a moment
I nearly believe
someone understands what we have just witnessed.

WILDING

1.

Running early through the mist,
in a field behind a dew-heavy lilac,
I saw a solitary doe stop grazing,
stand rigid silent as I loped by.
She never moved while I was in sight.

For the rest of that hour I ran
with wildness, saw the cougar's
rope-muscled back slide under
canopied mock orange, heard toucans
screech amid the fretful birdcall
of robins and wrens, ran with
a redfox grinning at my side.

Later, driving back to my city house,
I heard the newscaster say
peregrine falcons were hatching
on the high tops of buildings
in downtown Boston, Springfield, Albany,
falcons bred in captivity,
raised on those city roofs,
released, returning now to nest,
then soar, casting out over city streets,
a watchful eye gliding lightly over our heads.
This city has become their wild domain.

2.

Once we knew what was meant by wild—
the great beasts that prowled and killed
for food, not sport—the darkened green
of forest tangle where the unknown waits
for those who venture unaware
along the edge of safety—the lust or passion
that leaves us shaken in our own forest's midst.

But the cold touch of fear along my spine
comes now at times when I should count myself
safe—by anything I can measure.
Neighborhood streets, familiar paths.
Can these hold the shadow the falcon casts?

3.

I woke one night in Guatemala to mortar
shelling—a sudden thunder in the night,
a flare of light before the earth-shake.
I listened as the shells fell in the next
neighborhood, then slept again. Today
when someone asks, were you afraid? I answer yes,
but not of that. My memory holds another image—

> a woman nursing a sleepy fretting child,
> her own face heavy with wanting sleep,
> but she is a widow with three other children to feed.
> Dust from the coffee fields lies like white ash
> on her dark forearms.

4.

That woman running alone where she had run
so many nights before—stopped by blows,
raped, beaten, stabbed. The young black boy
looking for an address in a white suburb,
shot dead by strangers. A pregnant woman
leaving a childbirth class killed by her husband.

No acts of wildness these, not passion
nor bloodlust hunger. Such acts spring
from lack not surfeit. The empty heart,
the empty mind produce an empty rage that seeks
a sensate life to feed on.

This violence walks along our paths and sidewalks,
our everyday companion, not wildness:
drug-shot boys, death squad teams, men who program
death long distance, the order given then forgotten—
no wildness here, no wilderness to touch the soul,
no solitary walk into the greening unknown to find new life,
no search this for the fire breathed by mythical dragons.

GUATEMALAN PHOTOGRAPHS

for Gerardo

Each night in your dreams you rebuild
the rooms of the home you left behind.
You wake, dream again, and stand tangled
in the grass of a life that grew without you.

Your father took a picture off the wall
a photograph of his wife as a young woman,
the photo brown with age, the frame fly-specked—
turned it gently and removed the brown cardboard back
to show me, hidden behind, the photograph of your dead
brother, the oldest of his three sons,
who went to the university to become
a teacher but taught the wrong things,
who did not come home one night nor the next,
whose tortured body was dumped—not quite dead—
on a street near home, who fought for life
in the hospital and nearly lived,
but they came for him again
and this time his body was never found.

He told me this story
as we looked at the photograph
of a clear-eyed young man who smiled your smile
and then he turned his son's face down again,
closed the cardboard back.

This photograph can not hang in sight
because a neighbor might ask who is he? where is he?
and to have a son unaccounted is dangerous.

As he spoke, your mother—stooped with age
and illness—sat next to me, touching my hand
that had touched her son. She cried each time
I spoke your name. I asked, *por favor para Gerardo,
una fotografía?* She patted her hair and nodded.
They followed me out into the brightness of a small
courtyard where your father mends shoes

so they will have something to eat
and I turned their faces into the sun
for my camera.

And then I smiled into your last brother's
Smile—no photograph, but the image of you—
this handsome youngest son shook my hand warmly.
Somos hermanos, he shrugged when I complimented
his likeness to you. He lives with his two sons
in these same small rooms, works when he can,
and believes that Jesus is his friend;
therefore he will accept whatever Jesus gives him
unlike his brother—you, unnamed and unmourned—
who fled, who was wrong to want more in this life
now there is anger in his voice—
than two rooms and the company of fear.

The intensity, the slight glaze behind the eyes
would speak to me of madness, not anger,
except that this madness keeps him sane—
allows him to work each day in spite of the threats
the frequent moves to hide from the men who come
in darkglassed sedans to ask where his brother has gone,
allows him to hold his sons' hands as they cross the street
to catch the bus to school, to live in a room
next to his parents and wait each day
for the future to arrive.

> A world away I show you the photographs
> we took that day and watch you search
> for yourself in their faces, as if you lived
> a reversal of those ancient myths of souls
> who cannot rest until their bodies are buried.
> It is your body wandering restlessly across
> a frozen, snow-covered landscape waiting
> to reclaim your buried soul.

SANTA CRUZ DEL QUICHE

I have been in rooms where tension was a presence
alive and palpable, sitting like a well-muscled thug
in the center of the room. Those who spoke in spite
of the dangerous presence did so in low voices. Some
closed the windows first as if the thing were outside
instead of sitting there among us.

I have walked through dusty streets and caught
the surprised or furtive glances of those who knew
I did not belong, who thought they knew why I had come
the treacherous mountain roads winding across
the barranco and then up again, and this knowing made
me dangerous and few would speak.

I have sat in an open square in front of a yawning
cathedral entrance while children stood with their faces
in my face and stared at me with undisguised alarm
and glee. One watched the marks my pen traced across
the page, seeing nothing there but black on white for he
could not read English, Spanish or Quiche.

I squatted on my haunches in a corner one afternoon
watching a woman twist straw into a braid. Her fingers
moved without pause, a rhythm marking the conversation
that pulsed and slowed in the windowless room beyond.
Testimonies swelled and burst into life like the odor
of sweat and tears and straw in the room.

The son of Nicolas Mateo spoke:
My father works
in the finca. He was working in the field when
three hundred soldiers came. All day they went through
the coffee plants. That night they came to our hut
wearing soldiers clothes and black painted faces.
We were all sleeping. They kicked open the door.
My father was crying. They had a flashlight. My mother
saw when they took my father. He didn't have time
to put his shoes on. My mother hugged him.
They said if you don't come right now
we will kill you.

I breathed more slowly as the air in the room seemed
to die. Four times I heard the same story. Four men taken
at night. Four families were looking for a sign that someone,
anyone cared. They have stopped asking for reasons
or rescue. Nicolas Mateo. Luis Ruiz. Macario Pu Chivalan.
Agapito Perez Lucas. The present dead.

Heart Space

HEART SPACE

for Amelia Janet

This is no world for the faint
hearted, child, whose mother
dreamed you

while she watched the children
of other mothers play on a dirt floor
in a jungle village

and felt her heart jump
with fear as the children of other
mothers took rifles into the jungle

to train to live to be adults.
This is no world for the faint
of hope, woman

who dreamed
this child into life, who bore
and lost a daughter in one

breath. When we sat in your sun
filled kitchen, your belly
swollen with her

life, did we say to one another
it is we who are safe —
and feel

shame and relief at the space
between here and there
between us and them?

—the space of one heartbeat
was the lesson we learned
from your quickly

briefly known child.

STONE LIONS

In the quiet winter I jogged
around the oval for the first time,

delighted to find a footing
in that treachery of ice and snow.

I nodded to them then, the stone
lions guarding a driveway to nowhere,

relics of a mansioned life overlooking
the slow-moving Hudson where icefloes

packed tight into the shore. When
you walked the road with me,

water rushed over the rockfalls
into the stream, and chunks of broken

ice fled downriver. You pressed
a footprint into the last crusted

snow and for days I saw it there
as I loped around the circle, remembered

your moist breath on the raw air,
the tilt of your head as you greeted

my stone lions. Today there is green
tipping the ends of the branches,

spreading out over the brown groundcover,
tempting the deer to wanton acts

in search of grass, green nibbling
at the boundaries of my heart, as

the water rushes past restraint, over
the falls, races off ledges and banks,

as the heavy slate sky pushes down
pushes water out of the swollen earth

and in the new spring light
even the stone lions are greening.

THIS MOUNTAIN

I climb this mountain
a stranger seeking a foothold
in unfamiliar terrain although
heaven knows I'm no stranger
to the sweat and strain
the breath caught high
in an arching chest the heart
hammer ratcheting and starved
for oxygen and the long slow glow
of a descent after the summit.

      So I remind myself
I have done this before and take
comfort in what I know
while my eye searches for landmarks
to hold in memory landmarks
to hint the journey home
the way new lovers tell each other
again and again how they met
mark their coming together
creating answers in their telling
where there is as yet no question
stored against the day
when the question will matter
and when I pause in this climb
thinking only to breathe and rest
the moment stretches out

        into surprise
that I have come farther perhaps than I
had expected in this amount of time
for beneath me a hawk circles
above the clouds and this too
I have seen before and from just such
a vantage point and with such awe

but this mountain I remember
is unknown to me a countenance
I am learning newly and though
I have climbed many mountains
and feel their slopes familiar in my body
I have never been in this place before
and owe the process loving care
for I climb this mountain a stranger.

SILENCES

We talk of change
and separation,
how each new beginning

is preceded by loss.
The sun settles
behind a gray stone wall

as a gardener sprays
miracle gro across
the already deep green yard

and a cardinal splashes
crimson beneath the trees.
Your work here is finished

and yet you have ties
to this place, ties of heart
and history; the cardinal

hops closer. We listen
for his song, but he sits silent
on a branch over your head.

You turn toward me on the bench,
touch my arm and say it is good
to mark this passage

with an old friend who measures
the distance between yesterday
and tomorrow in her very

presence. Your hair falls
across your face and I reach
to stroke it—silky black

now half silvered, like mine—
the touch striking the heat
hidden deep in my belly

these many years and I know
I want more than this long-lived
friendship, want to be more

than the measure of your journey.
I lean toward you for a moment,
hesitate, and from the farthest

high corner of the courtyard
only the cardinal begins to sing.

CHILDHOOD'S END

---

for my father

I.

In death you do not look peaceful,
your chest arched for the last breath,
head thrown up to catch the air,
mouth open with the effort. Only
your eyes are closed.

You caught a fast track
toward death, surprising us all
with your single-minded sprint. Never
one to procrastinate, and yet when you died
your magazine subscriptions were paid
for two years in advance.

II.

On the second day of the new year
I hike high up into the Rincon Mountains,
hike beyond my strength, thirteen miles
up, past the desert, into the pines
where snow lies crusted in small pools,
drawn always by the promise of what lies
just a little further above Cow Head Saddle
around the bend from Helen's Dome up at
Manning Camp.

And then I have to go back down.

I have hiked beyond the daylight, worn out
even the sun, which flames down behind a western
range of mountains. City lights begin to glow
in the valley. Finally I flick on a small
flashlight and pick out the trail, rock by rock.

At the end I enter a valley, the dark desert
around me and above
                a mountain range of stars
blaze in the absence of the moon.

Last night in my dreams
I said goodbye to you over and over,
not a final goodbye, but everyday leave-takings,
a hug that means, I'll see you later.

III.

As the flesh wasted from your face,
your mother peered out at me,
she, twenty years older than you,
smiling the same smile, thinned with age.
When I look in the mirror, I am afraid
to smile; wrinkles crease my edges
as my hands crease and fold the clothes
you have shed.

For years I have contemplated old age as
an event for the future
today suddenly I
look over my shoulder and realize
I can't recall just when it arrived
though I can still see the doorway
it entered through.

IV.

At the bottom of the city
where Stone meets Sixth
I take the clothes
your wife and I have folded.
Down here homeless people
crouch in doorways. One woman
has taken a sterno stove
out of her backpack and is warming
lunch as though she were
in a wilderness of canyons and trees
instead of downtown buildings
and parking lots. I see faces
that look as if they have
folded in on themselves,
closed down, finished.

When does a life end
I wonder and by whose judgment?

V.

In an album
a photograph of you
a boy of twenty balancing
on one leg on a log washed by low waves.

Head thrown back,
your nervous grin of triumph
greets the camera, caught like a dream
that won't go away.

On that day you were ready for any dare.

You taught me how to sail when we both
were young, daring the waves in a salvaged
hull, daring the winds which
left us becalmed just at sunset.

Always there was one more wave to try,
one more improvement our small craft needed.
I learned more than sailing that year.
You taught me nothing is ever complete,
nothing is final.

VI.

High in the Rincons
in the shadow of Helen's Dome
snow ice melts porous in the sun
and freezes again in the night.

GRANDSON

He stands in front of me
legs wide arms open in a gesture
that seems to include the world
but only means to balance him.

He speaks a stream of syllables
caught in the perfect inflection of a question
and stops to wait for my response. I know
what he means, oh, not exactly

what he means but I can touch
the emotional center behind his wide-eyed
gaze and quizzical smile—I am here.
Are you here too? I nod and welcome him

this fifteen-month old grandson
who is risking language to tell us
what he feels and language—
make no mistake—is a risk and

whatever words he will learn whatever
articulation clarifies his tongue nothing
he ever says will be more clear
more necessary and more vulnerable

than this urgent heart felt baby talk.
We who are grown know the loneliness
of language, hide behind words, risking
nothing but losing everything

when we will not say to the world,
I am here. Are you here too?

Body of Love

BODY OF LOVE

I.

Entre la muerte y yo
he erigido tu cuerpo...
Rosario Castellanos

Because from the beginning you were fated
to be mine, because in the years before now,
apart, we learned the dance's movements, because
during these last long days I had stopped hoping,
but never ceased yearning, we came together
like the ocean meets a high cliff—crescendo
of foam on dark still waters beneath—and you
rest in my arms, a rock splashed by jubilant
waters.

Body of love, of lust, earthbound joy, festival
of taste, feast of smell, I burrow between
forked roots, wander with languid fingers
through crevices, at times a quiet stream
sliding, though not unnoticed, into your earth's
warm cave, at times the wild full river breaking
over banks of containment, flooding the swollen
plains, leaping from quiescence into the dangerous
unknown.

We know the spirit through these bodies, learn
ourselves by taste and smell, touch our inner
most souls with hands and tongues, exchange
permissions to be known—to allow another body
access, most holy terror, most longed for
and most feared—because of this,
this confirmation:
that I know myself immortal by the weight
of your earth on my chest.

II.

Incomplete people, that's what he called us,
those of us who love our own image in another.
*The only whole love, the only love God approves,
is between men and women. Nature intended—*
he pauses, searching for the image—*physical
complement between men and women, that is missing—*
he still gropes for words.

            It ought to give us pause,
this weighty disapproval from one who says he knows
what God and Nature mean.

But I know my own nature. Listen:

They call it love-making, what has happened
between the two people lying now in damp sleep
oblivious to the August sun high above the whispering
pines outside their bedroom window. Making love.
The whispered urgent yes, the look deep behind the eyes,
the opening,
breathless waiting for a touch that lingers everywhere
but there, there where she is waiting for more than fingers
lightly brushing back and forth, waiting for the smooth
silky warm first tongue touch. How is this love? This passion
that slides these two over the edge of self into a deep well
where they sink down and down, forgetting who is she and
who is she, forgetting time, that fiction which folds people
out of self, this effortless joining, this merging of tongues
and fluids, soft sighs, urgent cries? Could this make
love? Listen: Their hearts
have been changed by what has transpired, this breathing
into one another's souls started something growing,
something new that wasn't here before—a deepening,
some attitude, perhaps, which allows each to notice each
with a careful attention, with a joy that opens, opens,
letting in the sun.

III.

We climbed that mountain in the snow,
the three of us. Do you remember?
How our boots were soaked through
after the first half-mile, but we
slogged on, holding ourselves carefully
in the iced spots, thinking to show
your son the view from the windblown summit
of his first mountain.

We stopped at a waterfall, splashed with ice lace,
delicate as a snowflake, not quite concealing
deep and cold rushing water. I lined you up
for a picture, your son by your side, the gray
rock rising behind you. A winter perfect picture,
all tones of gray and white and dark mossy greens
in the water and pine trees, your son by your side,
his lean young body repeating yours. I paused
and looked around the camera to check this image,
then pressed the shutter. But the camera
took no picture.

We fussed with it briefly, then threw it
in the pack, shrugged, and went on climbing.
At the top we found only mist and dark clouds,
no amazing view to entice this boy to climb again.
Yet we had a wonderful day, do you remember?
He will not soon forget the climb, the summit
with no view, and I will remember a photograph
that exists only in me: that moment when I
looked around the camera and saw you,
saw winter close around your frosted skin,
saw dark water rushing through you,
saw your hand resting easily on your son's shoulder.

IV.

Catalina Mountains, Tucson, Arizona

We walked all afternoon with lightning
at our backs; it reached forward out of blackened
clouds to crackle whitely then fade into a thunder's
roar. We walked away from the mountain, down
the canyon basin, then out toward plains and houses,
a busy town. Ahead the sun pierced a too blue sky.
Behind? At every switchback we'd turn and check
the storm that followed, dark and grim,
then turn again and walk toward light.

My heart holds the image of our careful walk,
not headlong flight nor careless disregard,
but a steady pace, measuring the risk, and ready
to change direction if the lightning struck
too close—an image for life lived on an edge
but not beyond. And yet we love the chaos
of the storm, the fearful awe we feel when chains
of light connect sky high above these sharp
rock mountains—bare, bare rock that leaves
no place to hide.

Loving the walk, we court the storm. Loving
the storm, we permit the repetition of daily
life, those mundane moments stored, a bulwark
against the day when we will find ourselves
inside the storm, grasping with fear and fierce
will the sharp edge of a lightning strike.
What I know is this: love alone
will take us to that place.

V.

Will I still wonder
at hummingbird wings
that vibrate into shadows
when she has become as familiar to me
as the tree that draws her?

Will I feel
the vibration in my heart
when your fingers flutter
down my spine

my quickening joy when you
open the door after being away

when this life together
is what we expect?

I want to know

if the hummingbird
who hovers over my head each morning
during breakfast on the patio
will still be a miracle to me in ten years.

if your body warm with sleep
pressed close against my back after
the alarm has rung and been turned off

if the sound of your laugh
deep and full

if the shape of your jaw

the scent of your

the curve. . .

VI.

for Zoe

For eighteen years she walked with me, hiked
the northern woods and ran the path along the river,
moved when I moved, unperturbed, until that nameless
undefined thing, distinct as a heartbeat when it departs
but unnoticed when it remains, that slip of consciousness
that makes a personality, began to slide away and left
her shaken, confused, afraid in the most familiar place.

And so one day we walked her across the street
and held her while the vet shaved her leg
for the injection and I looked deep into her eyes
as they began to cloud over.

I walked away and left her there,
holding your hand, not fighting the tears.
Later we buried her ashes under a mesquite tree
where she had rested in the shade, still looking
—we imagined—for familiar shapes in this
unfamiliar desert land.

For a year we three walked out together, morning and night,
building a familiar life through the ritual she demanded.
This dog connected me to my other self, that young dreamer
of dreams no longer mine, who named a dog "life" as though
the naming of names could control life's events. Today
you and I walk together. I dream new dreams and wonder
what forever means, wonder whether love itself is like
that slip of consciousness because I know that love
can slide away, leaving only daily life and a vague
awareness of something that has been and I pray
that the rituals we create will protect us from this fate.

VII.

You wake at night, your sleep broken by sweat,
the tension slipping out of your skin like soft rain
damping the sheets. I wake at night to your waking
and to my own nightmares of torn bodies, photographs
of sawed off body parts, a head floating in a canal,
fished out by kids playing on the banks. My dreams
come from life, from newspapers and television reporting
the rape of the world, the tearing apart of the body
of life's normalcy as I understand it. Your sleep
is broken every hour. I dream broken bodies.

Two nights before the winter solstice, we light
the first candle on the Menorah. The small flame
trembles in the dark, calling for the return
of what? of light? — we know the days will lengthen
again after the solstice, the sun's power will warm
the days, shorten the night's fierce cold grip. This
will happen whether we light the candles or not,
so why do we repeat the words blessing the light,
why do we recreate this ritual from an older time
when omitting it meant the night might stay?

All evening our conversation circles around the 'whys',
the rape of women in Bosnia, the cold intentional
violence there—and in our own neighborhood a woman
raped and shot by three boys who wanted her car. "Why,"
one of them asked, "are you making such a fuss about it?
We didn't do anything much." The candles flame and die,
but the light will come again tomorrow night and again,
again. We wrap ourselves in the warmth of this home
we have created, and we know the 'why' of this.

VIII.

We hang a garland on the mesquite tree
red ribbons, someone's candy cane marked sock,
two green bottle pieces smoothed quarter size
are fished out of the creek and nestle
in a branch crook. The creek sparkles
diamonds in the sun as we light the mesquite
wood in the fireplace and prepare to cook.

You and I marvel at the unnatural sun
or so it seems to our northeastern eyes
and wonder how the ones we love and left behind
are spending this day. A cactus wren cackles
from deep within a bush, shadows of wind ruffle
the dry grass, and the creek rushes on, a constant
voice, company for the absent voices in my heart.

Two sit in the sand and talk, one wanders
into the brush, and I watch the others at the creek
pan gravel with a paper plate, looking for treasure
dropped from another time, another place. A magnet
pulls the iron fuzz into flower points, leaving behind
the tiny flakes of ruby garnet, dropped by the creek,
dark now with water, waiting, waiting, to be held up
to the light where the red heart of them will show.

Some jewels we choose with forethought, some we find,
gifts waiting at our feet, left by the pull and eddy
of the stream's rough dance, and yet the choice
is always ours to walk—or not—the path that winds
into the canyon. As the sun falls behind the high rock
walls we take the garland off the tree, scatter the cold
ashes from our fire, leave the green bottle glass eyes
to face the moon, and walk toward home.

IX.

I measure time by how a body sways.
Theodore Roethke

The geologic time line is gone, a white stripe
on a paved road into the canyon designed to make
earth time understandable to transient humans:
"Each step you take is about 50 million years."
The formation of this canyon began 2000 million
years ago; ten steps more on the ocean floor
and starfish swim across the rock, settle, die,
turn to mud, then rock, pushed down and down
by the weight of water.

This week the water roared
through the canyon, the creek that whispers soft
canyon music is swollen, pushing on the canyon walls,
tearing past the cottonwoods, rising, rising, the back
of a dinosaur pushing up through the earth. Roads
and bridges are gone. A cement block picnic table
floated downstream. Debris clogs the new ditches,
incipient canyons left by the stream. We walk the edge
of what was once a road with the others who have come
to see this bucking, buckling of the earth. Tourists

walk unsuspectingly back in time as the geologic line
unfolds without the map. Elbows flapping, children rise
to the surface of boulders, mouths open like fishes.
"The road got swallowed!" A man surveys the damage calmly,
"this isn't nearly as bad as the floods of '83." Heads nod
agreement and camcorders whir, recording this marker.
"Trust me," a woman insists to her companion.
"I've been buying chickens for forty years
and they're getting dirtier. Can you trust me on this?"

He shrugs, a communication earlier than speech.
We each mark our time by events that move us;
you and I struggle between joy at the stream's raw power,
sadness that we have lost a familiar road we've walked
through three seasons now. The waterfall that was dry
last month sprays our faces with fine mist. We ask
a stranger to take a picture, we two, our backs
to the falls, smile into the sun, as the water
roars words into silence.

X.

I follow your back through the fog
down a path winding through yellow
clouds of flowers. I had promised
you would see elk out here,
but ahead of us lies only a shrouded
beach, the tide pulled out to flatness.

We walk down to where a seal lies on the sand
flipping wetness onto its back. It peers
near-sightedly at us but does not leave,
perhaps could not leave. After a moment
we retreat. You seem unmoved.

Like cards being shuffled in a deck
images ruffle through my memory, layered,
shifting, merging with the deeper dream
that is always there, half hidden
behind the swaying kelp, waiting, waiting
to dart out, grab me, and then recede.

Crashing waves leapt high over rocks,
sucked the wind back down into the ocean,
at this place in my distant past. Then
she and I sat apart on the beach, each lost
in our own drama. "Look," I pointed
to the dainty elk grazing high in the dunes
among the cattle. She looked,
nodded, went back into her own thoughts.

In the fog you and I begin to drive away
when we see the elk antlers rising like ghost images
above the swirling mist. "Look," you point and stop
the car. We climb on the hood, peering into the disappearing
light as the antlers bob and wave, grateful to watch
for this moment.

We drive on and I know that
in this place I found something
I didn't know I was looking for,
just here where I had been searching
for something else.

XI.

for Mary Catherine

The abandoned garden circle
is empty at the center, gone to weeds
around the edge, brown the only blossoms

left from last year's harvest.
We are gathered for a darker harvest,
one that has interrupted daily life, moved us

away from the familiar
no easy transformation, this hard
pulling of life away from its center,

leaving her space empty.
She's here, we tell one another,
meaning it, meaning she is among us.

We don't lie and yet
it is not true. She was alone
in spite of our love, as she lived

alone in her body dying,
alone in her disease living. We,
living, believe we are not alone as we

stand casually among the fruit
of her harvested life, the children
she shaped, the house she built, the love

she cherished. And so we gather
in one last circle, shake her ashes

into the clear running stream, puff them
with our breath, dusty,
into the air, and let the last few sift
through our fingers into the mud around the base

of a new oak tree,
as late in June, too late for blossomings,
we planted Mary.

XII.

. . . the great dragons that used
to protect this land . . . have
now moved into another dimension.
Dhyani Ywahoo, *Voices of Our Ancestors*

The moon slows as it crests the canyon wall
like an athlete straining to reach the top
of a rock, hand over hand, anticipation
tensing and slowing each movement. We climb
deeper, higher, into the canyon, following
the shadow-gray road as moonglow bounces
off the top of boulders scattered in the stream
below us. Walking carefully in the half-light,
we are surprised when the moon strikes the road
at last and we emerge into a bright land without color.
I smell red dust and the scent of greenness floats up
from the stream banks where cottonwood trees
shudder in a faint breeze, but in this dimension
there are only shades of black, gray, and white.

On the lower flank of the canyon wall you show me
a large shadow, at night a dark opening, a cave
that is not there when we hike this road in day
light. We laugh and say, here is the entrance
to another world. Or perhaps we are in another
place and that is the entrance back into familiar
lands. You take my hand so that we will not stray
toward that dark gate. We are content with a fantasy
of a parallel time or place; this life is enough,
we say, walking through a craggy moonscape.
We do not need to lift the veil.

NOTES AND GLOSSARY

Taking Risks: the River Poems—the three rivers we risked during several summers were the Colorado, the Salmon, and the San Juan.

Crossing the Line—in January, 1994, the survivors of the Federal assault on the Branch Davidian religious compound were put on trial for killing Federal Agents. The trial was moved from Waco, Texas, site of the compound, to San Antonio. It was held in a court building only a few blocks from the historical Alamo where defenders of another era faced an assault by representatives of the Federal Government of Mexico. During the trial, a small replica of the Branch Davidian compound was a centerpiece in the courtroom. This replica was remarkably like that of the last defense of the Alamo, with General Santa Ana's army breaching the walls, which is on display at the Alamo.

Wilding: section 4—"that woman running alone…" refers to the Central Park assault on a jogger. Other references also are to current events, but their historical specificity is not important.

Santa Cruz del Quiche—this village in the highlands of Guatemala is in the area Rigoberta Menchu calls home. This incident occurred in 1989 during a long and intense decade of army violence against peasants and indigenous peoples. Finca—a plantation.

Body of Love: poem 1—Entre la muerta… "Between death and myself, I have placed your body."

Also available from Rising Tide Press:

	TITLE	AUTHOR	PRICE
❑	Agenda for Murder	Joan Albarella	11.99
❑	And Love Came Calling	Beverly Shearer	11.99
❑	By The Sea Shore	Sandra A. Morris	12.00
❑	Called to Kill	Joan Albarella	12.00
❑	Cloud Nine Affair	Katherine Kreuter	11.99
❑	Coming Attractions	Katherine Kreuter	11.99
❑	Danger! Cross Currents	Sharon Gilligan	9.99
❑	Danger in High Places	Sharon Gilligan	9.95
❑	Deadly Butterfly	Diane Davidson	12.00
❑	Deadly Gamble	Diane Davidson	11.99
❑	Deadly Rendezvous	Diane Davidson	9.99
❑	Dreamcatcher	Lori Byrd	9.99
❑	Emerald City Blues	Jean Stewart	11.99
❑	Feathering Your Nest	Leonhard/Mast	14.99
❑	Heartstone and Saber	Jaqui Singleton	10.99
❑	Isis Rising	Jean Stewart	11.99
❑	Legacy of the Lake	Judith Hartsock	12.00
❑	Love Spell	Karen Williams	12.00
❑	Nightshade	Karen Williams	11.99
❑	No Escape	Nancy Sanra	11.99
❑	No Witness	Nancy Sanra	11.99
❑	No Corpse	Nancy Sanra	12.00
❑	One Summer Night	Gerri Hill	12.00
❑	Playing for Keeps	Stevie Rios	10.99
❑	Return to Isis	Jean Stewart	9.99
❑	Rough Justice	Claire Youmans	10.99
❑	Shadows After Dark	Ouida Crozier	9.95
❑	Side Dish	Kim Taylor	11.99
❑	Storm Rising	Linda Kay Silva	12.00
❑	Sweet Bitter Love	Rita Schiano	10.99
❑	Taking Risks	Judith McDaniel	12.00
❑	The Deposition	Katherine Kreuter	12.00
❑	Tropical Storm	Linda Kay Silva	11.99
❑	Undercurrents	Laurel Mills	12.00
❑	Warriors of Isis	Jean Stewart	11.99
❑	When It's Love	Beverly Shearer	12.00

Please send me the books I have checked. I have enclosed a check or money order (not cash], plus $4 for the first book and $1 for each additional book to cover shipping and handling.

Name (please print)_____

Address_____

City _____State_____Zip_____

AZ residents, please add 7% tax to total.

RISING TIDE PRESS, PO BOX 30457, TUCSON AZ 85751

Rising Tide Press brings you the best in lesbian fiction and nonfiction. We publish books to stir the imagination for women who enjoy ideas that are out of the ordinary.

We are committed to our community and welcome your comments.

We can be reached at our website:
www.risingtidepress.com

More Fiction to Stir the Imagination
From Rising Tide Press

CLOUD NINE AFFAIR   Katherine E. Kreuter

Christine Grandy—rebellious, wealthy, twenty-something—has disappeared, along with her lover Monica Ward. Desperate to bring her home, Christine's millionaire father hires Paige Taylor. But the trail to Christine is mined with obstacles, while powerful enemies plot to eliminate her. Eventually, Paige discovers that this mission is far more dangerous than she dreamed. A witty, sophisticated mystery by the best-selling author of Fool Me Once, filled with colorful characters, plot twists, and romance.   **$11.99**

THE DEPOSITION   Katherine E. Kreuter

It is April in Paris and the Deposition's loopy narrator, G.B. is plotting the caper of capers. This provocative and hilarious novel by the author of the Paige Taylor Mystery Series resonates with gasps and guffaws.   **$12.00**

STORM RISING   Linda Kay Silva

The excitement continues in this wonderful continuation of TROPICAL STORM. Join Megan and Connie as they set out to find Delta and bring her home. The meaning of friendship and love is explored as Delta, Connie, Megan and friends struggle to stay alive and stop General Zahn. Again the Costa Rican Rain Forest is the setting for another fast-paced action adventure. Storm fans won't want to miss this next installment in the Delta Stevens Mystery Series.   **$12.00**

TROPICAL STORM   Linda Kay Silva

Another winning, action-packed adventure featuring smart and sassy heroines, an exotic jungle setting, and a plot with more twists and turns than a coiled cobra. Megan has disappeared into the Costa Rican rain forest and it's up to Delta and Connie to find her. Can they reach Megan before it's too late? Will Storm risk everything to save the woman she loves? Fast-paced, full of wonderful characters and surprises. Not to be missed.   **$11.99**

CALLED TO KILL   Joan Albarella

Nikki Barnes, Reverend, teacher and Vietnam Vet is once again entangled in a complex web of murder and drugs when her past collides with the present. Set in the rainy spring of Buffalo, Dr. Ginni Clayton and her friend Magpie add spice and romance as Nikki tries to solve the mystery that puts her own life in danger. A fun and exciting read.   **$12.00**

AGENDA FOR MURDER   Joan Albarella

A compelling mystery about the legacies of love and war, set on a sleepy college campus. Though haunted by memories of her tour of duty in Vietnam, Nikki Barnes is finally putting back the pieces of her life, only to collide with murder and betrayal.   **$11.99**

ONE SUMMER NIGHT   Gerri Hill

Johanna Marshall doesn't usually fall into bed with someone she just met, but Kelly Sambino isn't just anyone. Hurt by love and labeled a womanizer, can these two women learn to trust one another and let love find its way?   **$12.00**

BY THE SEA SHORE   Sandra Morris (avail 10/00)

A quiet retreat turns into more investigative work for Jess Shore in the summer town of Provincetown, MA. This page-turner mystery will keep you entertained as Jess struggles with her individuality while solving an attempted murder case.   **$12.00**

AND LOVE CAME CALLING   Beverly Shearer

A beautifully told love story as old as time, steeped in the atmosphere of the Old West. Danger lights the fire of passion between two women whose lives become entwined when Kendra (Kenny), on the run from the law, happily stumbles upon the solitary cabin where Sophie has been hiding from her own past. Together, they learn that love can overcome all obstacles.   **$11.99**

SIDE DISH   Kim Taylor

A genuinely funny yet tender novel which follows the escapades of Muriel, a twenty-something burned—out waitress with a college degree, who has turned gay slacker living into an art form. Getting by on margaritas and old movies, she seems to have resigned herself to low standards, simple pleasures, and erotic daydreams. But in secret, Muriel is searching for true love.   **$11.99**

COMING ATTRACTIONS
Bobbi D. Marolt

Helen Townsend reluctantly admits she's tried of being lonely...and of being closeted. Enter Princess Charming in the form of Cory Chamberlain, a gifted concert pianist. And Helen embraces joy once again. But can two women find happiness when one yearns to break out of the closet and breathe free, while the other fears that it will destroy her career? A delicious blend of humor, heart and passion—a novel that captures the bliss and blundering of love. $11.99

ROUGH JUSTICE
Claire Youmans

When Glenn Lowry's sunken fishing boat turns up four years after its disappearance, foul play is suspected. Classy, ambitious Prosecutor Janet Schilling immediately launches a murder investigation, which produces several surprising suspects-one of them, her own former lover Catherine Adams, now living a reclusive life on an island. A real page-turner! $10.99

NO CORPSE
Nancy Sanra

The third Tally McGinnis mystery is set aboard an Olivia Cruise. Tally and Katie thought they were headed out for some sun and fun. Instead, Tally finds herself drawn into a reunion cruise gone awry. When women start turning up dead, it is up to Tally and Cid to find the murderer and unravel a decades old mystery. Sanra fans new and old, won't be disappointed. $12.00

NO ESCAPE
Nancy Sanra

This edgy, fast-paced whodunit set in picturesque San Francisco, will keep you guessing. Lesbian PI Tally McGinnis is called into action when Dr. Rebecca Toliver is charged with the murder of her lover Melinda. Is the red rose left at the scene the crime the signature of a copycat killer, or is the infamous Marcia Cox back, and up to her old, evil tricks again? $11.99

NO WITNESSES
Nancy Sanra

This cliffhanger of a mystery set in San Francisco, introduces Detective Tally McGinnis, whose ex-lover Pamela Tresdale is arrested for the grisly murder of a wealthy Texas heiress. Tally rushes to the rescue despite friends' warnings, and is drawn once again into Pamela's web of deception and betrayal as she attempts to clear her and find the real killer. $9.99

DEADLY RENDEZVOUS
Diane Davidson

A string of brutal murders in the middle of the desert plunges Lt. Toni Underwood and her lover Megan into a high profile investigation, which uncovers a world of drugs, corruption and murder, as well as the dark side of the human mind. Explosive, fast-paced, & action-packed. $9.99

DEADLY GAMBLE
Diane Davidson

Las-Vegas-city of bright lights and dark secrets-is the perfect setting for this intriguing sequel to DEADLY RENDEZVOUS. Former police detective Toni Underwood and her partner Sally Murphy are catapulted back into the world of crime by a letter from Toni's favorite aunt. Now a prominent madam, Vera Valentine fears she is about to me murdered-a distinct possibility. $11.99

RETURN TO ISIS
Jean Stewart

It is the year 2093, and Whit, a bold woman warrior from an Amazon nation, rescues Amelia from a dismal world where females are either breeders or drones. During their arduous journey back to the shining all-women's world of Artemis, they are unexpectedly drawn to each other. This engaging first book in the series has it all-romance, mystery, and adventure. $9.99

ISIS RISING
Jean Stewart

In this stirring romantic fantasy, the familiar cast of lovable characters begins to rebuild the colony of Isis, burned to the ground ten years earlier by the dread Regulators. But evil forces threaten to destroy their dream. A swashbuckling futuristic adventure and an endearing love story all rolled into one.   • $11.99

WARRIORS OF ISIS
Jean Stewart

The third lusty tale is one of high adventure and passionate romance among the Freeland Warriors. Arinna Sojourner, the evil product of genetic engineering, vows to destroy the fledgling colony of Isis with her incredible psychic powers. Whit, Kali, and other warriors battle to save their world, in this novel bursting with life, love, heroines and villains. *A Lambda Literary Award Finalist* $11.99

EMERALD CITY BLUES
Jean Stewart

When comfortable yuppie world of Chris Olson and Jennifer Hart collides with the desperate lives of Reb and Flynn, two lesbian runaways struggling to survive on the streets of Seattle, the forecast is trouble. A gritty, enormously readable novel of contemporary lesbigay life, which raises real questions about the meaning of family and community. This book is an excellent choice for young adults and the more mature reader. **$11.99**

DANGER IN HIGH PLACES
Sharon Gilligan

Set against the backdrop of Washington, D.C., this riveting mystery introduces freelance photographer and amateur sleuth, Alix Nicholson. Alix stumbles on a deadly scheme, and with the help of a lesbian congressional aide, unravels the mystery. **$9.99**

DANGER! CROSS CURRENTS
Sharon Gilligan

The exciting sequel to Danger in High Places brings freelance photographer Alix Nicholson face-to-face with an old love and a murder. When Alix's landlady turns up dead, and her much younger lover, Leah Claire, the prime suspect, Alix launches a frantic campaign to find the real killer. **$9.99**

HEARTSONE AND SABER
Jacqui Singleton

You can almost hear the sabers clash in this rousing tale of good and evil, of passionate love between a bold warrior queen and a beautiful healer with magical powers. **$10.99**

PLAYING FOR KEEPS
Stevie Rios

In this sparkling tale of love and adventure, Lindsay West an oboist, travels to Caracas, where she meets three people who change her life forever: Rob Heron a gay man, who becomes her dearest friend; her lover Mercedes Luego, a lovely cellist, who takes Lindsay on a life-altering adventure down the Amazon; and the mysterious jungle-dwelling woman Arminta, who touches their souls. **$10.99**

LOVESPELL
Karen Williams

A deliciously erotic and humorous love story in which Kate Gallagher, a shy veterinarian, and Allegra, who has magic at her fingertips, fall in love. A masterful blend of fantasy and reality, this beautifully written story will delight your heart and imagination. **$12.00**

NIGHTSHADE
Karen Williams

Alex Spherris finds herself the new owner of a magical bell, which some people would kill for. She is ushered into a strange & wonderful world and meets Orielle, who melts her frozen heart. A heart-warming romance spun in the best tradition of storytelling. **$11.99**

FEATHERING YOUR NEST:
An Interactive Workbook& Guide to a Loving Lesbian Relationship

Gwen Leonhard, M.ED./Jennie Mast, MSW

This fresh, insightful guide and workbook for lesbian couples provides effective ways to build and nourish your relationships. Includes fun exercises & creative ways to spark romance, solve conflict, fight fair, conquer boredom, spice up your sex lives. **$14.99**

SHADOWS AFTER DARK
Ouida Crozier

While wings of death are spreading over her own world, Kyril is sent to earth to find the cure. Here, she meets the beautiful but lonely Kathryn, and they fall deeply in love. But gradually, Kathryn learns that her exotic new lover has been sent to earth with a purpose—to save her own dying vampire world. A tender, finely written story. **$9.95**

SWEET BITTER LOVE
Rita Schiano

Susan Fredrickson is a woman of fire and ice—a successful high-powered executive, she is by turns sexy and aloof. From the moment writer Jenny Ceretti spots her at the Village Coffeehouse, her serene life begins to change. As their friendship explodes into a blazing love affair, Jenny discovers that all is not as it appears, while Susan is haunted by ghosts from a past that won't stay hidden. A roller-coaster romance which vividly captures the rhythm and feel of love's sometimes rocky ride and the beauty of life after recovery. **$10.99**

Also by Judith McDaniel

Metamorphosis, Reflections on Recovery
Sanctuary, A Journey
The Stories We Hold Secret (coeditor)
Winter Passage
November Woman
Just Say Yes
Yes I Said Yes I Will
The Lesbian Couples Guide